# BONE BREAD

# BONE BREAD

poetry

J.B. Lain

Copyright © 2024 J.B. Lain
ISBN: 979-8-9911187-1-2
JBLW

# DEDICATION

For anyone still burning.

In all parts of the human body the Angel teaches us to consider their properties: concluding that since corporeal vision is an operation of the living body through a bodily organ, which devils lack, therefore in their assumed bodies, just as they have the likeness of limbs, so that have the likeness of their functions.But no difficulty arises out of what has been said, with regard to our principal subject, which is the carnal act which Incubi in an assumed body perform with witches: unless perhaps anyone doubts whether modern witches practise such abominable coitus; and whether witches had their origin in this abomination.

**From *Malleus Maleficarum* by Heinrich Kramer (1486), translated from its original Latin by Montague Summers (1928).**

# POEMS

Incense - 1
Offering - 3
Pact - 9
Bone Bread - 11
Invocation -15
Spell - 19

# WHAT FRUIT GROWS TO BE SLICED OPEN?

FROM WITHIN SHE
GNASHES ON
BONES THROWN
HER WAY

**Incense**

She growls in the night, flickering in firelight,
the ash above falling on her skin, still hot.

From within she gnashes on bones thrown her way;

a beast growing in the moonlight, stretching across her
belly, pale as the eyes that first seized her,
full and round, the village, burning,
turning her over and over on the spit.

She looks at the ash below,
spread over the soil as a shroud.

In time, what magic seeded?
What fruit grows to be sliced open?

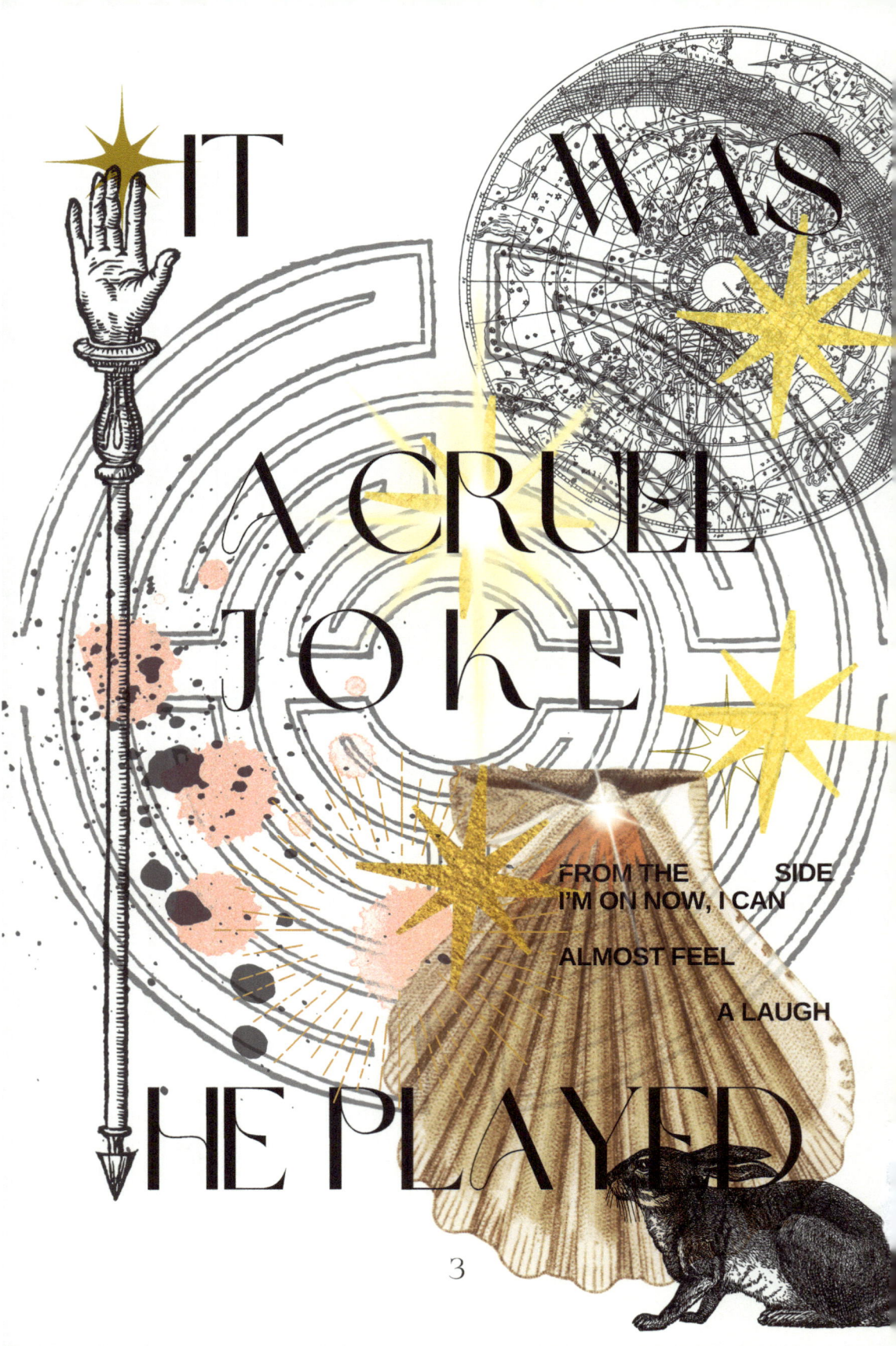

**Offering**

It was a cruel joke he played.
From the side I'm on now,
I can almost feel
a laugh somewhere inside my belly.

He showed me his cards many times,
and still I stayed. Until he finally played his hand.

It was a cruel joke.

Whenever I was out, he would draw
a tiny black dot on the floor by the bed.
Everyday he would slink away
to make the dot a little bit bigger,

by the tiniest of increments. Everyday.

At first I never even saw it.

But then the corners of my eyes would flutter
as I left the bed each morning.
Nothing the matter, really, until it stayed behind my
eyelids.

Is it growing?
Maybe he tracked in mud on his boots.
Maybe I spilled some paint.

I tried to scrub it away, but it would always reappear the
next day.
Darker and slightly bigger.
Always growing, day after day.

He denied he could even see the mark
upon the floor beside the bed.

In time, I became obsessed with the dot.

In time, it grew to a spot, which then became
a rather large hole.

I scrubbed until my fingers bled, but still it stayed. And
grew.

All the while he denied seeing anything
upon the floor beside the bed.

First it claimed the cats.

Then came the night when it was large enough
to fit a me-sized thing within it,

which was the day I fell
through the hole in my floor.

I was never heard from again.

**Pact**

Bending down, kissing cloven feet,
shouldn't be shocked
when kicked in the teeth.

Spreading bone and blood in the mud reserved
for burying the ones
that should have known better.

Spreading legs, smearing blood
'round the grave reserved
for burying his bone.

The arching back, the spit, the rack,
this offering spins atop a funeral pyre
cooking in the shepherd's desire
to burn his little sheep.

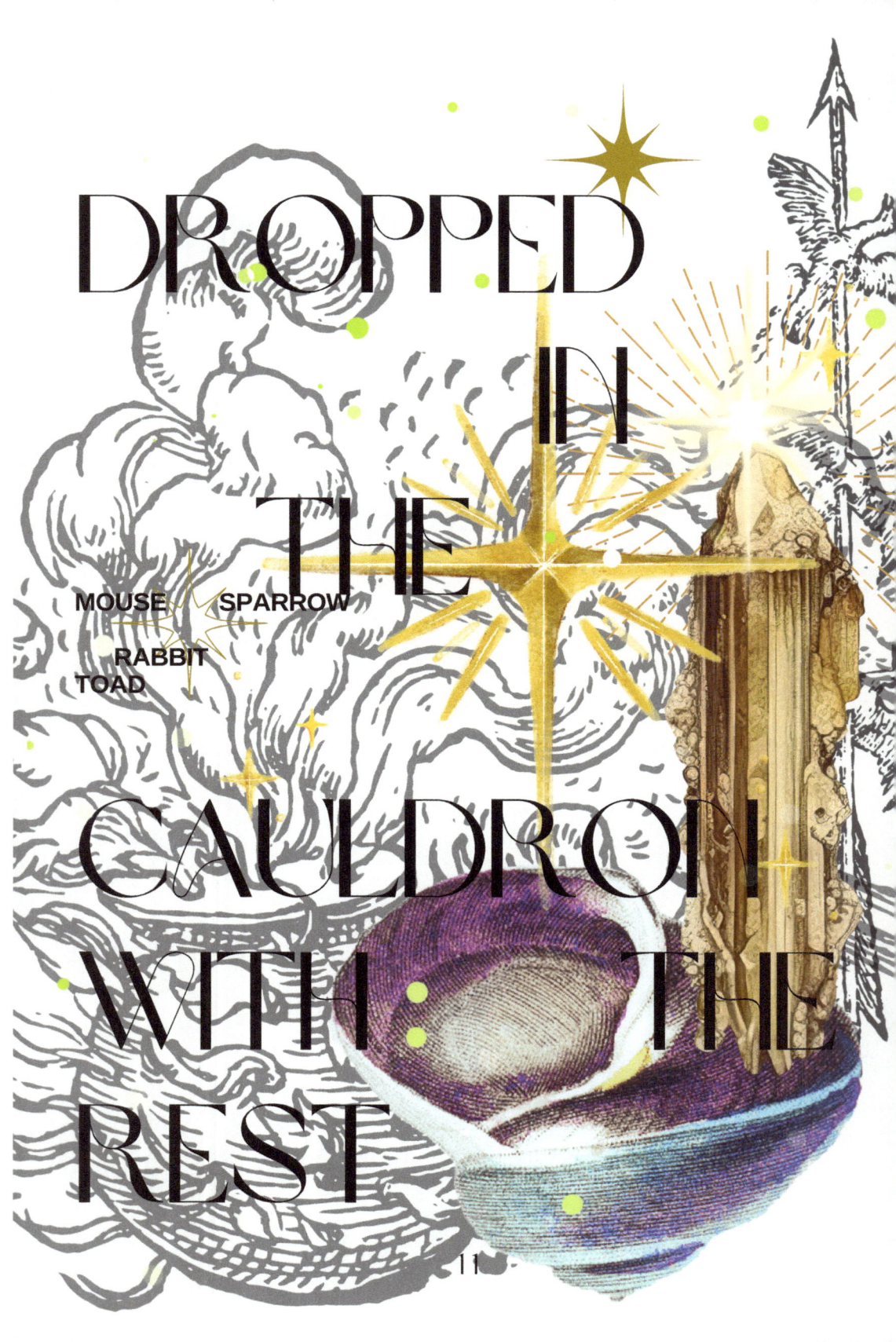

# DROPPED IN THE CAULDRON WITH THE REST

MOUSE  SPARROW
RABBIT
TOAD

**Bone Bread**

She wore rags of remarks, briar slashed and a pile of burs
plucked out of heels and ankles and toes.

Each one could have been a man.

On his boots he tracked no ordinary mud, a sludge of what
the cat didn't cover on her way out. And what she dragged
in,

dropped in the cauldron with the rest, stirred
thrice widdershins,
to be spilled over booted footfalls.

Though his hounds bay upwind,
her little kitties keep their game:
mouse, sparrow, rabbit, toad.

All make the descent:
plop, plop, plop, plop.

How much more of him will fit down there?
And how many servings will he make?

When the bone bread rises in the flames,
his soul is hers to take.

# FOR THE FLOOD WAS HER CRECHE

NOT UNICORN, NOR DRAGON, NOR GRIFFIN, NOR MAN.

**Invocation**

Alluvial, forgotten,
but never washed away,
for the flood was her creche.

Not unicorn, nor dragon, nor griffin, nor man.

She was a boss-ass bitch treading flood waters,
waiting millennia after millennia.

She's grinning now gill to gill
because the drought is coming
sooner than planned.

She still has legs though her toes be webbed,
and when she and the time comes
she will walk endless miles
across dusty drained-ocean plains,

without looking back
at the bloody trail she leaves behind.

Each drop of her heat springs forth
an oasis of new creatures sprouting,
singing beastly hymns:

All hail the glory of the Merbitch!

**Spell**

The moon doesn't part the clouds;
the gape is parted from below.

I didn't ask the moon for anything,
only waited for it to wax.

Here's where the spell can begin:

I bound my hands beside my bed,
Prayed the Devil take my head.
From the village three times fled,
Cast me out and eat my bread.

Now bring me stories while I sleep,
Show me She who calls the deep.
Because I could not stop for thee,
Her soggy carriage waits for me.

# ABOUT THE AUTHOR

J.B. Lain is a poet, suburban witch and all around chill dude. She holds a master's degree in Creative Writing from Texas State University. She lives in San Antonio, Texas where she works as a communications professional, but she's striving to become moss in her next life.

www.ingramcontent.com/pod-product-compliance
Lightning Source LLC
Chambersburg PA
CBHW042303150426
43196CB00005B/68